CLUE BOOKS

Flowerless Plants

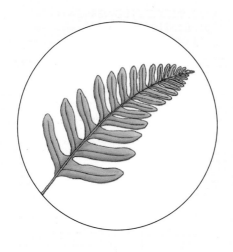

Gwen Allen   Joan Denslow

OXFORD UNIVERSITY PRESS

Oxford University Press, Great Clarendon Street, Oxford OX2 6DP

Oxford New York
Athens Auckland Bangkok Bogotá Bombay
Buenos Aires Calcutta Cape Town Dar es Salaam
Delhi Florence Hong Kong Istanbul Karachi
Kuala Lumpur Madras Madrid Melbourne
Mexico City Nairobi Paris Singapore
Taipei Tokyo Toronto

and associated companies in
Berlin Ibadan

Oxford is a trade mark of Oxford University Press

© Oxford University Press 1997
First published 1970
New edition 1997

CLUE BOOKS – FLOWERLESS PLANTS
produced for Oxford University Press
by Bender Richardson White, Uxbridge

Editors: Lionel Bender, John Stidworthy Design: Ben White
Media Conversion and Page Make-up: MW Graphics
Project Manager: Kim Richardson
Original artwork: Tim Halliday
Additional artwork: Ron Hayward

A CIP catalogue record for this book is available from the British Library

ISBN 0-19-910176-0 (hardback)   ISBN 0-19-910182-5 (paperback)

1 3 5 7 9 10 8 6 4 2

Printed in Italy

CONTENTS

ABOUT THIS BOOK

This book is about flowerless plants. It allows you to identify the most common flowerless plants of northern and western Europe and it also tells you a little about their life cycle. Flowerless plants can be found in gardens, parks, woods and on roadsides and coasts.

The book is divided into seven main units, one for each major group of flowerless plants. Within each unit are three sections: Introduction, Clues and Identification. The Introduction tells you the main features and growth pattern of the plants.

The Clues section allows you to identify each flowerless plant you have found. The arrows and numbers in the right-hand margin tell you which page to go to next.

The Identification section consists of colour plates illustrating the individual types or species. Most types of flowerless plant you find will be illustrated in this section. Alongside each illustration is the plant's common name, its scientific or Latin name (in *italic* type) and a basic description of it. Measurements are given in millimetres or centimetres, abbreviated to mm or cm (1 cm = 10 mm = 2/5th inch).

The coloured band at the top of each double-page spread helps you locate the relevant sections of the book: *blue* for Introduction, *yellow* for Clues, *red* for Identification. An arrowhead at the top right of a spread shows the topic continues on to the next spread. A bar at the top right indicates the end of that topic.

This book is about flowerless plants.

These plants do not produce flowers or seeds, but grow from spores which are produced in **FRUITING BODIES**.

If your plant looks like one of these, turn to the pages shown.

In order to name your plant you will need to use the clues.

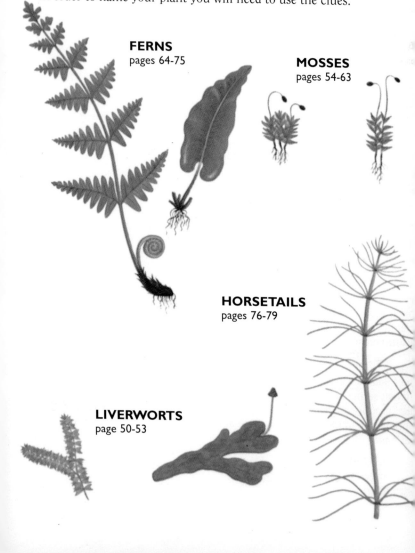

FERNS
pages 64-75

MOSSES
pages 54-63

HORSETAILS
pages 76-79

LIVERWORTS
page 50-53

The size of each plant is given in centimetres by each major coloured illustration through the rest of the book.
If no measurement is given, the illustration is life-size.

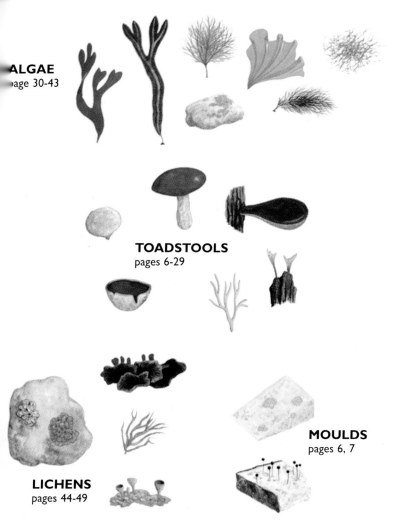

ALGAE
page 30-43

TOADSTOOLS
pages 6-29

MOULDS
pages 6, 7

LICHENS
pages 44-49

MOULDS AND TOADSTOOLS

Moulds and toadstools belong to the group called **FUNGI**. The fungus body is a mass of white threads called **HYPHAE** which grow and feed on dead plant and animal remains. The mass of hyphae produces **FRUITING BODIES**, which are the parts we most often see and call moulds and toadstools.

Look for toadstool hyphae among rotten leaves and dead wood. Put some on a glass slide and look at them under a microscope.

leaf

white hyphae

MOULDS

Moulds are very small fungi. Their spores float in air or water. Some swim. Collect as many moulds as you can from cheese, bread, fruit and other things, or grow some.

fruiting bodies

blue or white powdery fruiting bodies

hyphae in bread

fruit

cheese

HOW TO GROW MOULDS

You will need a piece of bread and a clean plastic dish with a lid. Put the bread in the dish, pour on enough water to make it wet, and leave it in the room for half an hour to allow the spores from the air to fall on it. Put the lid on and leave it in a warm place. You should be able to see the fruiting bodies after a few days.

MOULD FRUITING BODIES

In order to see moulds more clearly, use a needle or tweezers to separate a small quantity. Put it on a glass slide, and examine it under a microscope. The fruiting body may look like these.

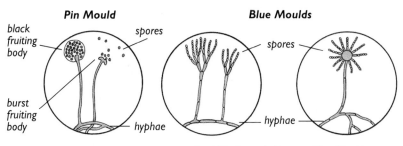

penicillin is made by some Blue Moulds

TOADSTOOL SPORES

The colour of a toadstool's spores can help you tell what kind it is. You may be able to see spores if you put a thin gill of an Agaric (see page 8) or a scraping from the inside of a Cup Toadstool (see page 28) on a glass slide and look at it under a microscope.

Another way of looking at spores is to make a **SPORE PRINT**. To do this, find a fully grown Agaric Toadstool which is still fresh. Cut off the stem and put the cap, gills downwards, on a piece of paper. Cover it with a box or jar to keep it free from draughts, and leave it overnight. Next morning carefully remove the box and cap: the spores will have fallen from the gills and made a print on the paper.

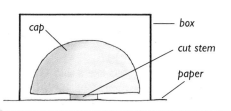

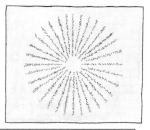

ALWAYS wash your hands after collecting or touching toadstools. DO NOT eat them unless you have checked with an expert that they are edible.

8 CLUES TO TOADSTOOLS

CLUE A | If the fruiting body has a cap with gills underneath, on which the spores (see page 7) grow, it is a **GILLED MUSHROOM** or **TOADSTOOL** (Agaric).

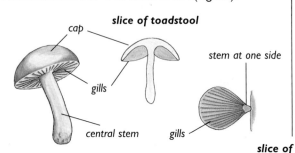

slice of toadstool

cap

gills

central stem

gills

stem at one side

CLUE B | If the fruiting body has a thick, spongy cap with tubes underneath, in which the spores grow, it is a **SPONGE TOADSTOOL** (*Boletus*).

slice of toadstool

cap

tubes

central stem

CLUE C | If the fruiting body grows on trees, has tubes underneath in which the spores grow, and most often looks like a bracket or a shelf, it is a **BRACKET TOADSTOOL** (Polypore).

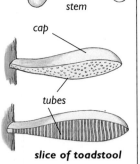

cap

tubes

slice of toadstool

CLUE D | If the fruiting body grows on wood, looks like a thin crust or bracket or shelf, but does not have tubes underneath, it is a **SKIN TOADSTOOL** (Thelophore).

JE E

If the fruiting body is more or less cup-shaped, with smooth or frilly edges, it may be a **CUP TOADSTOOL** *(Peziza)*, **HORN OF PLENTY** *(Craterellus)* or **JELLY TOADSTOOL**.

 21, 28

JE F

If the fruiting body looks like this and smells strongly of rotten meat, it is a **STINKHORN**.

 27

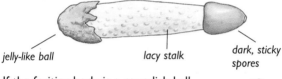

jelly-like ball   *lacy stalk*   *dark, sticky spores*

JE G

If the fruiting body is a roundish ball

 27

E H

If the fruiting body is slender, leathery and has one or more branches that may be flattened or club-like at the ends

 28

In order to name your gilled Toadstools you need to know the colour of their spores, because they are grouped according to their spore colour.
The gills are most often the same colour as the spores, but you should check this by making a spore print (see page 7).

CLUE A

If the spores are white, cream, pale yellow, pale pink or pale violet, go to **CLUE B.**

If the spores are deep pink

If the spores are rusty-brown

If the spores are purple or black

CLUE B

If the stem is very short and grows on one side, it is a **BRACKET AGARIC.**

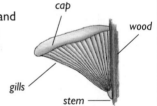

If the stem is central and the gills grow down the stem (decurrent)

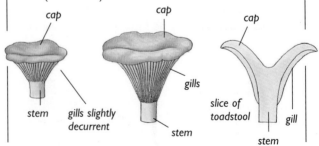

CLUE B
continued

If the stem is central and the gills are not decurrent, go to **CLUE C**.

slices of toadstools

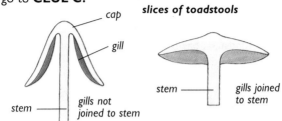

cap

gill

stem

gills not joined to stem

stem

gills joined to stem

CLUE C

If the toadstool has both a ring and a volva (frilly base), it is an *AMANITA* (poisonous).

cap

gills

fleshy ring

frilly base (volva)

 16

If the toadstool has a ring but no volva, it may be a **PARASOL MUSHROOM** *(Lepiota)* or a **HONEY TOADSTOOL** *(Armillaria)*.

cap

gills

fleshy ring

 18, 19

If the toadstool has a volva but no ring, it is a **GRISETTE**.

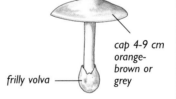

cap 4-9 cm orange-brown or grey

frilly volva

(not illustrated elsewhere in this book)

If the toadstool has neither a ring nor a volva, go to **CLUE D** overleaf.

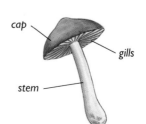

cap

gills

stem

CLUE D

If the toadstool has a cap, stem and gills of the same yellowish-red or violet colour, it may be *LACCARIA*.

If the toadstool has thick, waxy gills and often a slimy cap, it may be a **WAX CAP** *(Hygrophorus)*.

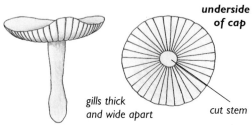

gills thick and wide apart

underside of cap

cut stem

If the toadstool has firm brittle gills all the same length, it may be a *RUSSULA*.

underside of cap

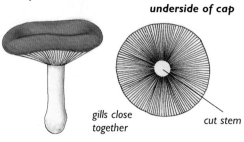

gills close together

cut stem

If the toadstool has gills of different lengths and a tough, firm (not stringy) stem greater than 5 mm in diameter, it may be a *TRICHOLOMA*.

underside of cap

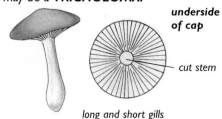

cut stem

long and short gills

If the toadstool has a tough stringy (fibrous) stem, and the edge of the cap rolls inwards, it may be a **SHANK TOADSTOOL** *(Collybia)*.

20

cap — / — rolled edge

— stringy stem

If the toadstool has a thin stem (less than 5 mm in diameter), a soft, thin conical cap through which the gills may be seen, and is not rolled inwards at the edge, it may be a
STRIPED BONNET
(Mycena).

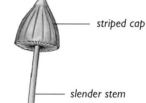

— striped cap

20

— slender stem

If the toadstool is tough and leathery when dry, and the cap, which becomes more or less flat, often rolls inward at the edge, it may be a **MARASMIUS.**

20

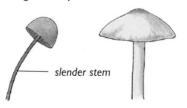

— slender stem

14 CLUES TO AGARICS – 2

CLUE A

If the stem is short and grows to one side of the cap, it may be a **BRACKET AGARIC** (*Crepidotus*).

underside of cap

gills

branch

stem

If the stem is in the middle or a little to one side and the gills grow down the stem (decurrent), it may be **PAXILLUS.**

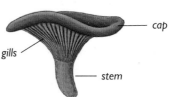

cap

gills

stem

If the gills are not decurrent, and there is a ring on the stem, it may be **PHOLIOTA.**

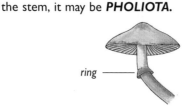

ring

If the toadstool has neither a ring nor decurrent gills, but has a cobweb-like veil beneath the cap when young, it may be a **VEIL TOADSTOOL** (*Cortinarius*).

cap

cobweb-like veil

If the toadstool does not look like these

JE B If the gills grow down the stem (decurrent) and the cap becomes cup-shaped with frilly edges, it is **THE MILLER** (*Clitopilus*).

 23

If the cap is thin, most often striped, and shaped like a Chinese hat, it is a **CHINESE HAT TOADSTOOL** (*Rhodophyllus*).

 23

If the toadstool does not look like these, it may be a **FAWN** *PLUTEUS*.

 23

JE C If the gills and cap become ragged, soft and inky, it is an **INKCAP** (*Coprinus*).

young inkcap

older inkcap

ragged edge

 24

If the toadstool has a ring, it may be a **MUSHROOM** (*Agaricus*) or a **VERDIGRIS TOADSTOOL** (*Stropharia*).

ring

 25

If the toadstool does not look like any of these

 23, 25

Blusher
(Amanita rubescens)
(cap 6–12 cm)
woods, July–Oct
turns red when bruised

poisonous

Scarlet Flycap
(Amanita muscaria)
(cap 6–16 cm)
birch and pine woods
Aug–Nov

looks very
like *deadly
poisonous*
Death Cap

False Death Cap
(Amanita phalloides)
(cap 5–9 cm)
beech, oak and conifer woods
July–Nov

Blackening Russula
(Russula nigricans)
(cap 10–20 cm)
mixed woods. Aug–Nov

Milk-White Russula
(Russula delica)
(cap 6–12 cm)
mixed woods
Sept–Nov

poisonous

Sickener
(Russula emetica)
(cap 6–9 cm)
under conifers
Aug–Nov

edible

Common Russula
(Russula xerampelina)
(cap 5–12 cm)
woods Aug–Nov
smells of crab

Deceiver
*(Laccaria
laccata)*
(cap 1–6 cm)
woods
July–Dec

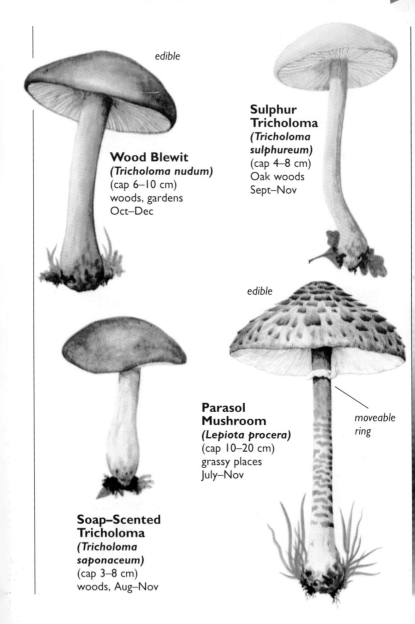

edible

Wood Blewit
(Tricholoma nudum)
(cap 6–10 cm)
woods, gardens
Oct–Dec

Sulphur Tricholoma
(Tricholoma sulphureum)
(cap 4–8 cm)
Oak woods
Sept–Nov

edible

Parasol Mushroom
(Lepiota procera)
(cap 10–20 cm)
grassy places
July–Nov

moveable ring

Soap–Scented Tricholoma
(Tricholoma saponaceum)
(cap 3–8 cm)
woods, Aug–Nov

Scarlet Wax Cap
(Hygrophorus coccineus)
(cap 2–5 cm)
in grass near woods
July–Dec

edible

edible

Honey Toadstool
(Armillaria mellea)
(cap 3–10 cm)
on trees
July–Dec

edible

Parrot Wax Cap
**(Hygrophorus
psittacinus)**
(cap 1–3 cm)
short grass,
copses
July–Nov

Buff Wax Cap
**(Hygrophorus
pratensis)**
(cap 2–7 cm)
grasslands
Aug–Dec

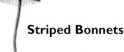

Striped Bonnets

(Mycena vitalis)
(cap 1–5 cm)
on buried twigs
July–Jan

(Mycena flavo-alba)
(cap 1–5 cm)
short grass
Aug–Nov

Spindleshank
(Collybia fusipes)
(cap 3–8 cm)
base of trees
May–Dec

Wood Woolly Foot
(Collybia peronata)
(cap 2–5 cm)
woods
Aug–Nov

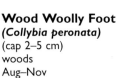

**Fairy Ring
Marasmius**
(Marasmius oreades)
(cap 2–6 cm)
short grass,
often in rings
July–Nov

**Horsehair
Marasmius**
(Marasmius androsaceus)
(cap 1 cm)
conifer needles,
twigs. May–Nov

edible

Twig Marasmius
(Marasmius ramealis)
(cap 1 cm)
dead twigs
June–Oct

A milky juice appears when the toadstool is broken

edible

edible

Slimy Milk Cap
(Lactarius blennius)
(cap 4–10 cm)
beech woods. Aug–Nov
juice turns grey

Saffron Milk Cap
(Lactarius deliciosis)
(cap 4–10 cm)
under conifers. Aug–Nov
juice turns carrot-coloured

No milky juice appears when the toadstool is broken

poisonous

edible

edible

**Common
Funnel Cap**
(Clitocybe rivulosa)
(cap 2–4 cm)
in short grass, often in
rings with Fairy Ring
Marasmius Aug–Nov

Horn of Plenty
*(Craterellus
cornucopioides)*
(5–12 cm tall)
among leaves in woods
Aug–Nov. Easily dried

Chanterelle
*(Cantharellus
cibarius)*
(cap 3–10 cm)
woods
July–Dec

edible

Fairy Cake Hebeloma
(Hebeloma crustuliniforme)
(slimy cap 3–7 cm)
damp soil in
woods, gardens
Aug–Nov

poisonous

Changeable Pholiota
(Pholiota mutabilis)
(cap 3–6 cm)
woods
April–Dec

Scurfy Tubaria
(Tubaria furfuracea)
(cap 1–3 cm)
on soil and sticks
in gardens, parks,
fields and woods
Jan–Dec

Brown Cone Cap
(Conocybe tenetra)
(cap 1–3 cm)
grassy places, woods
May–Dec

Veil Toadstool
(Cortinarius elatior)
(cap 4–9 cm)
beech woods
Aug–Oct

Paxillus
(Paxillus involutus)
(cap 5–12 cm)
mixed woods
Aug–Nov

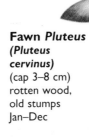

Fawn *Pluteus*
***(Pluteus
cervinus)***
(cap 3–8 cm)
rotten wood,
old stumps
Jan–Dec

**Chinese Hat
Toadstool**
***(Nolanea
cericeus)***
(cap 2–6 cm)
short grass
May–Oct

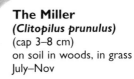

The Miller
(Clitopilus prunulus)
(cap 3–8 cm)
on soil in woods, in grass
July–Nov

AGARICS – PURPLE–BLACK SPORES

**Common
Brittle Cap**
***(Psathyrella
gracilis)***
(cap 2–6 cm)
densely tufted
on or near
tree stumps
Aug–Nov

Crumble Cap
(Coprinus disseminatus)
(cap 0.5 cm tall)
clustered round old stumps
May–Nov

Common Ink Cap
(Coprinus atromentarius)
(cap 3–7 cm tall)
fields, gardens, often
clustered at base
of trees
Aug–Dec

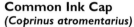

Brittle Ink Cap
(Coprinus plicatilis)
(cap 0.5–1.5 cm tall)
grassy places, roadsides
May–Nov
stem is brittle

*edible
when fresh*

Shaggy Ink Cap
(Coprinus comatus)
(cap 5–12 cm tall)
fields and roadsides
May–Nov

Verdigris Toadstool
(Stropharia aeruginosa)
(cap 2–8 cm)
grassy places June–Nov

Field Mushroom
(Agaricus campestris)
(cap 4–8 cm)
grasslands
Aug–Nov

ring ——

edible

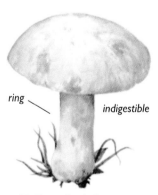

ring

indigestible

Yellow-Staining Mushroom
(Agaricus silvicola)
(cap 4–10 cm)
grassy places
Aug–Nov
stains yellow when broken

Sulphur Tuft
(Hypholoma fasciculare)
(cap 3–7 cm)
tufts on stumps
Jan–Dec

Boletus lutea
(cap 5–10 cm)
in grass under conifers
Aug–Nov

edible

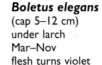

Boletus elegans
(cap 5–12 cm)
under larch
Mar–Nov
flesh turns violet
when broken

edible

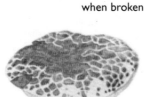

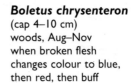

Boletus chrysenteron
(cap 4–10 cm)
woods, Aug–Nov
when broken flesh
changes colour to blue,
then red, then buff

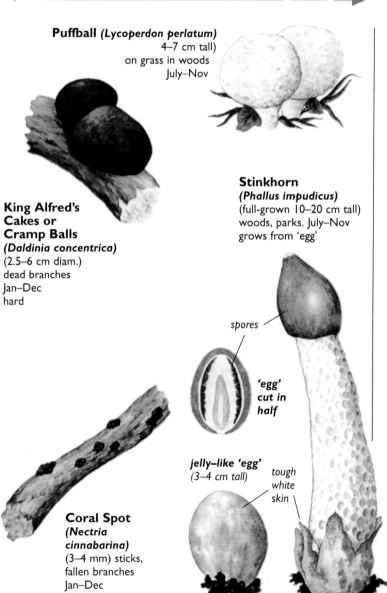

Puffball *(Lycoperdon perlatum)*
4–7 cm tall)
on grass in woods
July–Nov

King Alfred's Cakes or Cramp Balls
(Daldinia concentrica)
(2.5–6 cm diam.)
dead branches
Jan–Dec
hard

Stinkhorn
(Phallus impudicus)
(full-grown 10–20 cm tall)
woods, parks. July–Nov
grows from 'egg'

spores

'egg' cut in half

jelly–like 'egg'
(3–4 cm tall)

tough white skin

Coral Spot
(Nectria cinnabarina)
(3–4 mm) sticks,
fallen branches
Jan–Dec

CLUB–LIKE TOADSTOOLS

Candle Snuff
(Xylaria hypoxylon)
(2–6 cm tall)
on dead wood
Jan–Dec

CLUB TOADSTOOLS

*Clavaria
cristata*
(2–5 cm tall)
in woods
Aug–Dec

*Clavaria
corniculata*
(2–6 cm tall)
in grass
June–Dec

JELLY TOADSTOOLS
(feel jelly-like)

**Yellow Brain
Toadstool**
(Tremella mesenterica)
(10–20 cm across)
dead branches
Jan–Dec

Jew's Ear
(Auricularia auricula)
(3–10 cm across) on elder wood
Jan–Dec

CUP TOADSTOOLS

**Orange
Peel** *(Peziza aurantica)*
(1–12 cm across)
grass or soil in woods, edges
of paths. Nov–Jan

Scarlet Elf Cap
(Peziza coccinea)
(2–6 cm across)
dead wood. Dec–Mar

BRACKET TOADSTOOLS (POLYPORES)

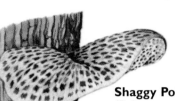

Shaggy Polypore
(Polyporus squamosus)
(10–30 cm across)
elm and ash trunks
April–Oct

Polystictus
(Trametes versicolor)
(3–5 cm across)
stumps and branches
Jan–Dec

Birch Polypore
(Piptoporus betulinus)
(5–30 cm across)
birch trees
Jan–Dec

BRACKET AGARICS

SKIN TOADSTOOLS (THELOPHORES)

on dead branches

Stereum purpureum
(1–3 cm
across)

Soft Slipper Toadstool
(Crepidotus mollis)
(1–5 cm)
on wood. July–Nov
spores rusty brown

Oyster Mushroom *edible*
(Pleurotus ostreatus)
(3–17 cm)
on trees
Jan–Dec
spores pale lilac

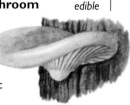

Algae are green plants that have neither leaves nor roots. They grow on old fences, tree trunks, wet soil, in fresh and sea water.
Collect as many different algae as you can: if they are small, mount some in a drop of water on a glass slide and look at it under a microscope.

If the plant is green, and grows on fences, trees, wet soil, or in fresh water it may be a powdery or a filamentous alga.

If the plant is green and powdery, it may be a **POWDERY ALGA**. (See also Lichens, page 44.)

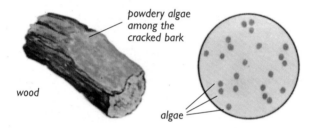

powdery algae among the cracked bark

wood

algae

If the plant is made up of green threads called filaments, it is a **FILAMENTOUS ALGA,** often called **BLANKET WEED.**

Spirogyra
slimy threads,
green spiral

Vancheria
long green tubes

green
network

star-shaped
green spots

If you wish to know more about green algae you will need to look in other books (see page 80).

If the plant is red, brown or green and grows in the sea or on the seashore it is a **SEAWEED.**

Seaweeds cling with a holdfast to rocks and other weeds on the seashore.

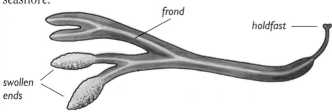

frond

holdfast

swollen ends

The leaf-like parts of the plants are called **FRONDS**. Like other plants, seaweeds contain a green pigment called **CHLOROPHYLL**, which is needed for making food from sunlight and air. They also have brown and red pigments that help them to trap more of the light that reaches them through the water. If you put some seaweed in a dish and pour boiling water on it, the red or brown pigment will ooze out, leaving the green pigment in the frond. Spores (see page 4) may grow in swollen ends of fronds or in special fruiting bodies which burst when ripe. The spores escape into the sea, settle on rocks or other seaweeds, and grow into new plants.

special fruiting body

holdfast

HOW TO MOUNT SEAWEEDS
Press medium or large seaweeds dry, and cover them with clear self-adhesive plastic. In order to mount small seaweeds you will need to float out small pieces in a saucer of sea water. (The colour may fade if you use tap water.) Slip a piece of paper underneath the weed and lift it carefully out of the water, keeping the weed spread out over the paper. When the paper and weed have dried, cover with clear self-adhesive plastic. Add it to your collection. Label it.

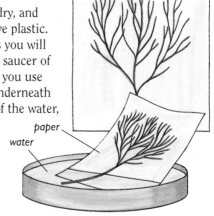

paper

water

CLUE A   If it is a green seaweed go to **CLUE B.**
If it is a brown seaweed go to **CLUE C.**
If it is a red seaweed

CLUE B   If the seaweed frond is like a large, thin leaf, it may be
SEA LETTUCE (*Ulva*).

If the seaweed is a mass of unbranched, tubular
fronds, it may be ***ENTEROMORPHA.***

If the seaweed is a mass of very fine, thread-like
branched fronds, it may be ***CLADOPHORA.***

JE B
inued

If the seaweed is thick and branched, and feels velvety and spongy, it is *CODIUM.*

 43

E C

If the frond is very large, single, sometimes divided at the end, and has a branched holdfast, it is an **OARWEED** *(Laminaria).*

 37

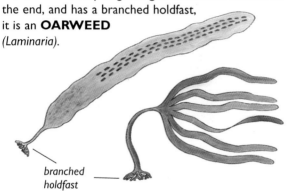

branched holdfast

If the frond is large, branched (always dividing into two at each branch) and has a flattened holdfast, it may be a **WRACK** *(Fucus).*

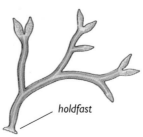

holdfast

38

(Clue C continued overleaf)

CLUE C
continued

If the fronds are slender, stiff and branched, it may be **SHRUBBY SEAWEED** (*Cystoseira*).

If the fronds are very fine, thread-like and grow on rocks or other seaweeds, it is either *ECTOCARPUS* or a **TUFTED BROWN SEAWEED.**

If the fronds look like one of these

Bubble Seaweed
(*Leathesia*)

Bootlace Seaweed
(*Chorda*)

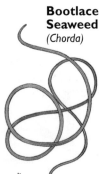

slimy bunches

Peacock Tail
(*Padina*)

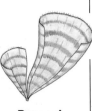

E A

If the fronds are leafy, it may be **LAVER** *(Porphyra)* or **DULSE** *(Rhodymenia)*.

40, 41

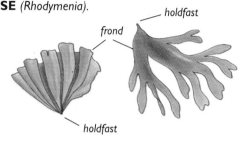

holdfast

frond

holdfast

If the fronds are rather stiff and flat, it may be *LAURENCIA* or **CARRAGHEEN** *(Chondrus)* or *GIGARTINA*.

40

If the fronds are cylindrical, jointed and soft, it may be *LOMENTARIA*.

41

If the fronds are hard and coral-like, or form flat, hard patches on stones, and the chalky covering dissolves in vinegar, it is a **CORALLINE SEAWEED**.

41

Corallina officinalis

stone

Lithophyllum

If the fronds are divided into numerous slender branches

42

Bootlace
(Chorda filum)
(180–600 cm long)
lower shore

Shrubby Seaweed
(Cystoceira)
(30 cm long)
often iridescent,
in clumps in rock pools,
lower shore

Ectocarpus
(2–15 cm long)
in clumps, on rocks
and seaweeds all over
the shore

Bubble Seaweed *(Leathesia)*
(3–4 cm across)
on rocks and seaweeds, middle
and lower shore March–Sept

Peacock Tail
(Padina)
(5–15 cm)
lower shore

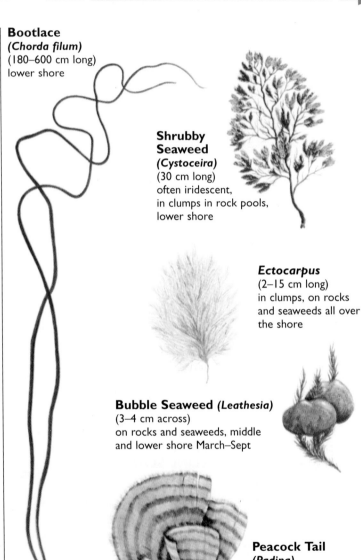

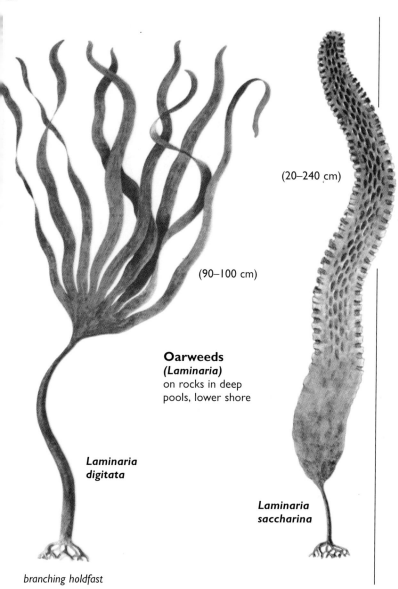

(20–240 cm)

(90–100 cm)

Oarweeds
(Laminaria)
on rocks in deep
pools, lower shore

*Laminaria
digitata*

*Laminaria
saccharina*

branching holdfast

WRACKS – on all rocky shores

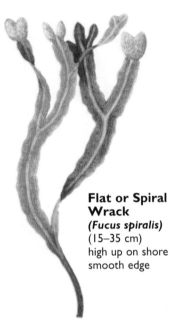

Flat or Spiral Wrack
(Fucus spiralis)
(15–35 cm)
high up on shore
smooth edge

Channelled Wrack
(Pelvetia canaliculata)
(10–15 cm)
high up on shore
edges curled to form
a hollow channel

Tufted Brown Seaweeds
middle and
lower shore on
other seaweeds

Elachista
(2–3 cm)

Sphacelaria
(2–3 cm)

Toothed Wrack
(Fucus serratus)
(30–100 cm)
middle and lower shores
toothed edge

Bladder Wrack
(Fucus vesiculosus)
(30–90 cm)
on exposed middle shores
smooth edge
paired bladders

Knotted Wrack
(Ascophyllum nodosum)
(40–100 cm)
middle shore in sheltered bays
single bladders

Middle and lower shore in rock pools

Laurencia
(7–10 cm)
mat-like covering
on rocks

Laver *(Porphyra)*
(12–24 cm)
fried and eaten as laver
bread in South Wales

Gigartina
(10–20 cm)

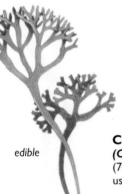

edible

Carragheen
(Chondrus)
(7–15 cm)
used for jellies

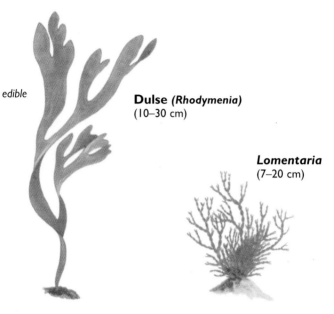

edible

Dulse *(Rhodymenia)*
(10–30 cm)

Lomentaria
(7–20 cm)

CORALLINE SEAWEEDS

Encrusting Coralline
(Lythophyllum)
(5–8 cm)
on rocks over most
of the shore

Corallina
(5–10 cm)
middle shore

There are very many fine, red seaweeds; those illustrated are some of the most common ones.

Middle and lower shores in rock pools

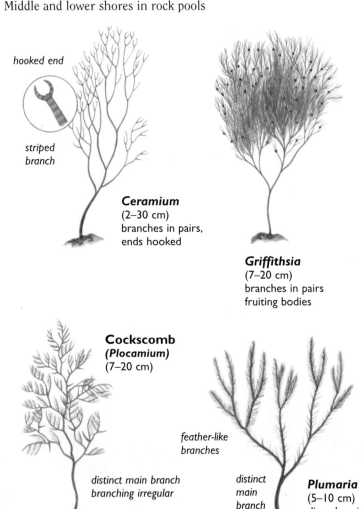

hooked end

striped
branch

Ceramium
(2–30 cm)
branches in pairs,
ends hooked

Griffithsia
(7–20 cm)
branches in pairs
fruiting bodies

Cockscomb
(Plocamium)
(7–20 cm)

feather-like
branches

distinct main branch
branching irregular

distinct
main
branch

Plumaria
(5–10 cm)
dingy hanging
tufts

High or middle shores

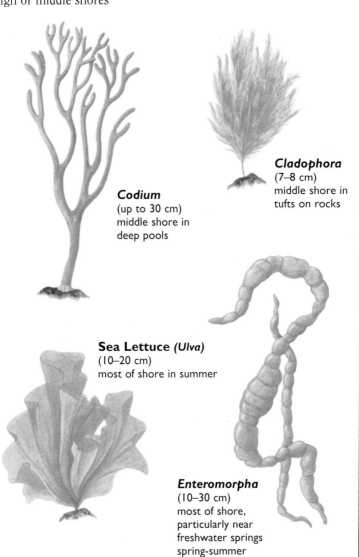

Codium
(up to 30 cm)
middle shore in
deep pools

Cladophora
(7–8 cm)
middle shore in
tufts on rocks

Sea Lettuce *(Ulva)*
(10–20 cm)
most of shore in summer

Enteromorpha
(10–30 cm)
most of shore,
particularly near
freshwater springs
spring-summer

Lichens are most often greyish–green plants that grow on rocks, stones, roofs, soil, trees and bushes. Many are used to make dyes.

Collect as many different kinds as you can. If they are powdery, scrape a small quantity of powder on to a glass slide and look at it under a microscope. If they are leafy, put a small piece on a glass slide, look first at the upper side and then the lower under a microscope. Break the leafy part, called the **THALLUS**, and look carefully at the broken edge.

You will see that the lichen thallus is really made up of two plants growing together to make one. Most of the thallus is made up of white fungal threads or **HYPHAE** (see page 6). Among the hyphae numerous minute algae grow (see page 30).

Lichens are able to grow where other plants would die, because the algae make the food, and the fungus provides the water by soaking it up when it rains.

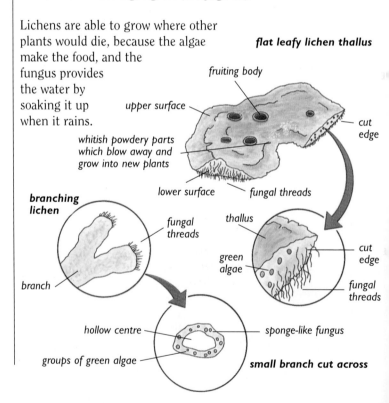

flat leafy lichen thallus

fruiting body

upper surface

cut edge

whitish powdery parts which blow away and grow into new plants

lower surface   fungal threads

branching lichen

fungal threads

branch

thallus

green algae

cut edge

fungal threads

hollow centre

sponge-like fungus

groups of green algae

small branch cut across

UE A | If the lichen thallus forms a greyish-green, blackish, or orange crust on stone or wood, it is an **ENCRUSTING LICHEN.**

wood

 46

IE B | If the lichen thallus is greyish-green, blackish, or orange, flat, leaf-like, and grows over wood, stones or soil it is a **FLAT LEAFY LICHEN.**

 48

IE C | If the greyish-green, leaf-like thallus is rather small and covered with fruiting bodies that look like one of these, it is a **CUP LICHEN** (Cladonia).

fruiting bodies

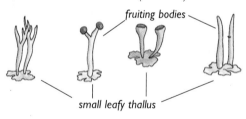

small leafy thallus

49

IE D | If the greyish-green leafy thallus is branched, and most often attached by a holdfast to rocks or branches, it is a **BRANCHING LICHEN**.

 47

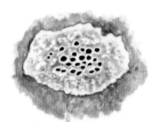

Wall *Lecanora*
on rocks and walls

Black Shields
(*Lecanora*)
on rocks and walls,
especially by the sea

Lecidia
wall tops, bricks

Scattered *Lecanora*
on limestone, concrete,
mortar

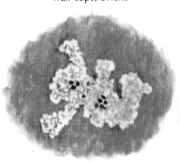

Scribble Lichens
on trees

Pertusaria pertusa

*Graphis
scripta*

Beard Lichen *(Usnea)*
on trees

Evernia
flattened thallus whose
upper and lower surfaces
look different
on trees and fences

Ramalina
flattened thallus whose upper
and lower surfaces look alike
on trees and fences

Branching *Cladonia*
clumps on heaths

Dog-tooth Lichen
(Peltigera)
on soil

Parmelia
on trees,
fences, rocks

Physcia
most often forms
circular clusters
on trees, walls

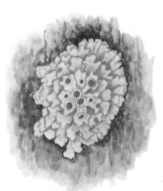

**Yellow Scales
Lichen** *(Xanthoria)*
stones, roofs

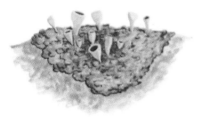

**Common Cup Lichen
(*Cladonia*)**
walls, tree stumps

Slender *Cladonia*
peaty heaths, peaty soil,
tree trunks

Red-Topped *Cladonias*
heaths

Liverworts often grow in wet places on stream banks and in woods. The leaf-like part, which is very green, is called a **THALLUS**. Small plants can be mounted in a drop of water and looked at under a lens or microscope.

Spores (see page 4) grow in fruiting bodies (capsules) under a protective covering. They burst when ripe. Slender, spring-like **ELATORS** help to scatter the spores, which grow into a thallus if they fall on wet places. If you look at a burst capsule under a microscope (see below) you will see spores and elators.

Some liverworts produce both spores and tiny bud-like parts called **GEMMAE**. The gemmae fall to the ground and quickly grow into new plants. Try to grow gemmae by putting a few on damp soil in a container.

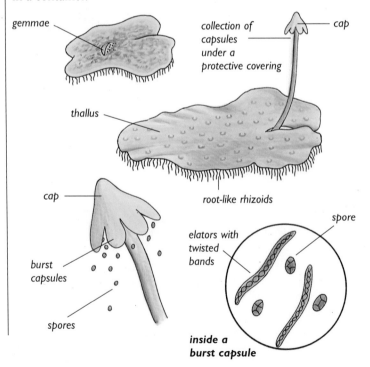

gemmae

collection of capsules under a protective covering

cap

thallus

cap

root-like rhizoids

burst capsules

spores

spore

elators with twisted bands

inside a burst capsule

A | If the thallus is large and leaf-like (see illustration page 50)

 52

B | If the thallus is very small, has flat, leaf-like parts, without midribs, and all the cells are roundish (see below), it may be a **LEAFY LIVERWORT**.

 53

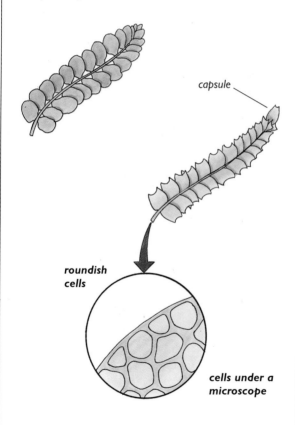

capsule

roundish cells

cells under a microscope

(See also Flat Fork Moss, page 59, **CLUE E.**)

Thallus large and leaf-like

Crescent Cup Liverwort *(Lunularia)*
(1.5–2.5 cm long)

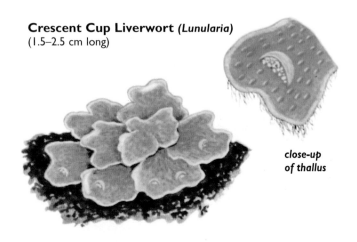

*close-up
of thallus*

Great Scented Liverwort
(Conocephalum)
(10–20 cm long)

Leafy Liverworts or Scale Mosses

close-up of leaf-like parts

Lophocolea bidentata
often mixed with mosses on woodland bank

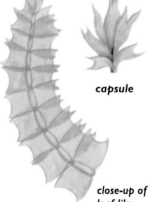

capsule

Lophocolea crispitata
on decaying tree stumps, shady banks and moist walls

close-up of leaf-like parts

Moss plants are small. Their leaves grow close together on a slender stem. They most often grow in masses in damp shady places. The spores of mosses grow in fruiting bodies called **CAPSULES**.

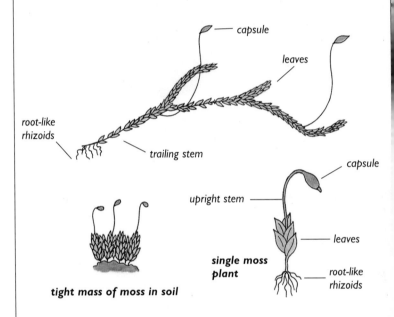

tight mass of moss in soil

single moss plant

Make a collection of as many different moss plants as you can. You will sometimes find several different kinds in one clump. Mount them on card under clear self-adhesive plastic. Label them. If the plants grow in tight clumps, use two large pins or needles to separate them before you mount them.

If you are mounting long trailing mosses, mount them so that you can see how they branch. This will help you when you are trying to name them.

trailing moss mounted and labelled

MOSS CAPSULES

Look at a moss capsule under a microscope or lens with good magnification. If it has a cap and lid, pull them off; on the end of the capsule you will see the teeth which open in dry weather so that the spores from inside can be shaken out by the wind, and blown to new ground where they will grow.

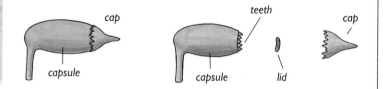

Try to shake or squeeze some spores out of the capsule. Watch what happens to the teeth of a dry capsule when you put a drop of water over it.

MOSS LEAVES

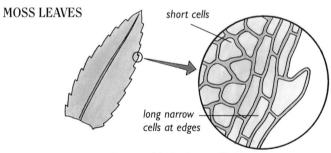

see also page 56 clue B and 58–59 clue E

Look at the leaves of moss plants under a microscope. The box-like structures you can see are cells. You can see them in moss leaves because they are arranged in a single layer, but in fact all plants and animals are made up of minute cells. The leaves of different mosses have differently shaped cells.

Examine each plant carefully.

CLUE A

If the plant has long, trailing, branched stems that spread out over the surface on which it grows, go to **CLUE B.**

If the plant grows upright and is most often unbranched, go to **CLUE C.**

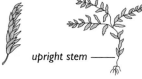

tree-like branching at top

upright stem

CLUE B

If the plant grows in spongy masses in wet places, most often has branches arranged in pairs around the stem, and has both green and colourless cells in the leaf, it is a **BOG MOSS** (*Sphagnum*).

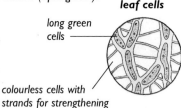

leaf cells

long green cells

colourless cells with strands for strengthening

If the branches of the plant are not arranged in pairs, and most of the leaf cells are long and narrow, it may be **WILLOW MOSS** or one of the **FEATHER MOSSES.**

long, narrow cells

⌐E C | If the plant is very small (2 cm or less), grows in dense patches and has a hair-like point or pale tip on its leaves, it may be a **DWARF MOSS** or **SILVERY THREAD MOSS**: go to **CLUE D**.

one leaf

hair-like point

If all the plants grow in loose patches, the leaves are without hair-like points and a single plant can easily be separated from the rest

 58 E

E D | If the plant has tightly overlapping leaves and grows in silvery patches on seaside cliffs, on pavements or wall tops and in other man-made habitats, it may be **SILVERY THREAD MOSS**.

⮕ **63**

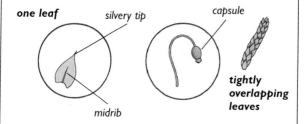

one leaf *silvery tip* *capsule*

midrib

tightly overlapping leaves

If the hair-like point, which may be colourless, is long, and the plant has a short capsule with short, straight teeth, it may be **CUSHION MOSS** (*Grimmia* group).

⮕ **63**

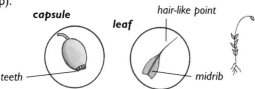

capsule *leaf* *hair-like point*

teeth *midrib*

CLUE D
continued

If the hair-like point is long, and the plant has a long capsule with twisted teeth, it may be a **SCREW MOSS** (*Tortula* group).

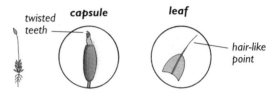

twisted teeth · *capsule* · *leaf* · hair-like point

If the plant is similar to a Screw Moss, but the hair-like point is short and the capsules have pale yellow stalks, it may be a **BEARD MOSS** (*Barbula* group).

leaf · short hair-like point

CLUE E

If the plant forms whitish-green spongy lumps, grows in woodlands or on wet moors, and the leaves have both green and colourless cells, it may be **WHITE FORK MOSS** (*Leucobryum*).

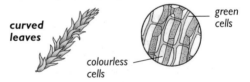

curved leaves · green cells · colourless cells

If the plant is tall (5–15 cm), the leaves grow loosely along the stem, and each leaf has a colourless base, it may be a **HAIR MOSS** (*Polytrichum* group).

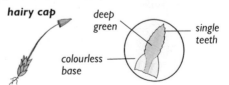

hairy cap · deep green · single teeth · colourless base

E E
:inued

If the plant is similar to a Hair Moss, but the leaf is all green, it may be **WAVY LEAVED THREAD MOSS** (*Atrichum*).

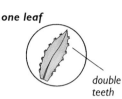

one leaf

double teeth

 62

If the upper leaves form a rosette, the capsule is bent and the cells of the leaf are almost rectangular, it may be a **CORD MOSS** (*Funaria*).

bent capsule

leaf cells

rosette of leaves

 62

If the leaves are flattened, arranged in two rows along the stem and have a small 'pocket' near the base of each leaf, it may be a **FLAT FORK MOSS** (*Fissidens* group; see also Leafy Liverworts, page 51).

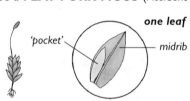

one leaf

'pocket'

midrib

 62

If the plant is not like any of these, has leaf cells which are more or less square, except round the edges, where they may be long, and a capsule which droops, it may be a **THREAD MOSS** (*Bryum* and *Mnium* groups).

 63

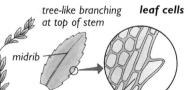

tree-like branching at top of stem

leaf cells

midrib

upright stem

leaf

long cells at edge of leaf

Circles show close-ups of leaves and
capsules.

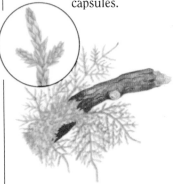

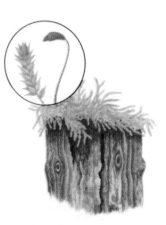

Fern-like Feather Moss
(Plagiothecium denticulatum)
woods, shady banks

Rough-Stalked
Feather Moss
(Brachythecium rutabulum)
in woods, on stones, tree
stumps, branches
and lawns

Cypress-Leaved
Feather Moss
**(Hypnum
cupressiforme)**
wall tops, boulders,
logs, soil in woods
and gardens

Willow Moss
**(Fontinalis
antipyretica)**
on stones or wood
in slow-flowing
streams or lakes

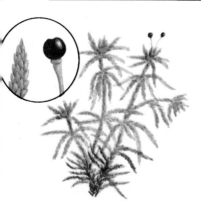

Common Bog Moss
(Sphagnum palustre)
(12–20 cm long)
bogs

Red Bog Moss
(Sphagnum rubellum)
(7–30 cm long)
on top of bog moss
tussocks

Beard Moss
*(Barbula
convoluta)*
(1 cm)
bare ground,
wall tops

Wall Screw Moss
(Tortula muralis)
(less than 1 cm tall)
bricks and stones
everywhere

Cord Moss
*(Funaria
hygrometrica)*
(3–10 mm)
bare soil in fields, gardens,
woods particularly after fires

Common Hair Moss
(Polytrichum commune)
(5–10 cm) woods, hedge banks

Wavy-Leaved Thread Moss
(Atrichum undulatum)
(2–5 cm)
shady banks, woods

White Fork Moss
(Leucobryum glaucum)
(3–10 cm, cushions up to
1 metre) woodlands, heaths

Flat Fork Moss
(Fissidens bryoides)
(1–1.5 cm)
shady banks

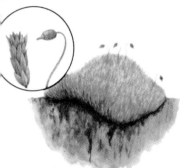

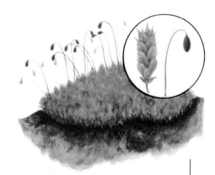

Grey Cushion Moss
(Grimmia pulvinata)
(1–1.5 cm) walls

Greater Matted Thread Moss
(Bryum capillare)
(2–5 cm) walls, roofs, fences

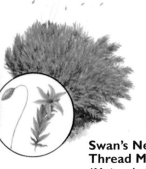

Palm Tree Moss
(Mnium undulatum)
(6–8 cm)
grassy banks,
woodlands

Swan's Neck Thread Moss
(Mnium hoznum)
(2–4 cm)
woodlands

Silvery Thread Moss
(Bryum argenteum)
(1–1.5 cm)
silvery grey patches on
seaside cliffs, pavements,
roofs and wall tops

Ferns are green plants with large leaves called **FRONDS**. The fronds are deeply divided into leaflets called **PINNAE**. A pinna may be divided again into **PINNULES**.

The young fronds grow coiled up at the end of the short underground stem.

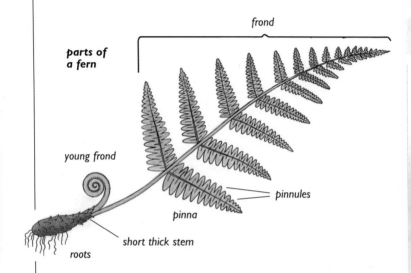

parts of a fern

frond

young frond

pinnules

pinna

short thick stem

roots

It is illegal to dig up wild ferns, but you may collect part of a frond from each plant. You can buy fern plants from nursery gardens.

Collect as many different kinds as you can.

If you are mounting a collection of ferns, turn some of the pinnules over to show the clusters of spore cases (see page 65).

During the summer and autumn the spore cases grow in clusters on the underside of the fronds. They may be protected by a cover.

In order to name your ferns you will need to look closely at the arrangement and shape of the clusters of spore cases. Use a magnifying lens or microscope.

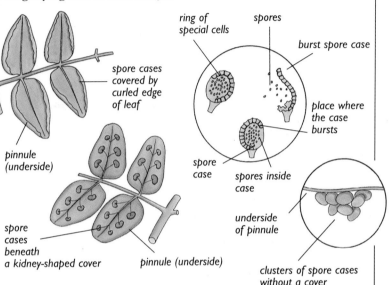

spore cases covered by curled edge of leaf

pinnule (underside)

spore cases beneath a kidney-shaped cover

pinnule (underside)

ring of special cells

spores

burst spore case

place where the case bursts

spore case

spores inside case

underside of pinnule

clusters of spore cases without a cover

HOW TO GROW FERNS

It is possible to grow ferns from spores that you collect from both wild and cultivated plants, but it may be several months before small fern plants can be seen.

You will need a clear plastic box or glass butter dish with a lid, half full of damp soil or peat. Shake the ripe spores onto the soil, put the lid on and leave in a light place.

In spring you may find tiny plants growing in soil around bigger fern plants.

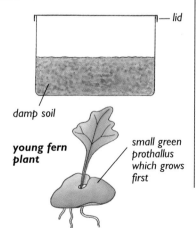

lid

damp soil

young fern plant

small green prothallus which grows first

CLUE A

If the spore cases grow on special fronds that look like this, it is **ROYAL FERN** (Osmunda).

part of frond with spore cases

part of leafy frond

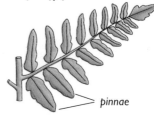

pinnae

If the spore cases grow on special fronds in the centre of the plant, and the fronds look like this, it is **HARD FERN** (Blechnum).

frond with spore cases

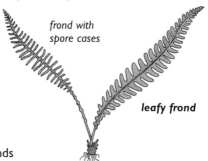

leafy frond

If all the fronds look alike see **CLUES B, C** and **D** below.

CLUE B

If the frond is single, it is either **HART'S TONGUE FERN** (Phyllitis) or **BIRD'S NEST SPLEENWORT.**

part of underside

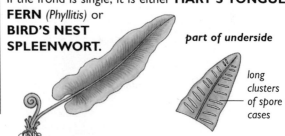

long clusters of spore cases

UE B
tinued

If the fronds have slender wiry black stems, it is
MAIDENHAIR FERN.

 73

*tips of leaves
curved
over spore
cases*

If the fronds look like this, and the spore cases grow
along the edges, which are curved over them, it may
be **RIBBON FERN** (Pteris).

 71

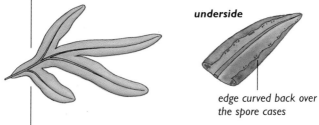

underside

*edge curved back over
the spore cases*

If the fronds appear branched, grow to 200 cm tall,
and have several large, divided pinnae widely
separated on a strong, shining frond stalk, it is
BRACKEN.

 72

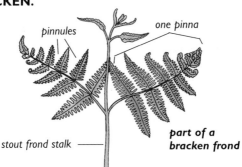

pinnules

one pinna

stout frond stalk

**part of a
bracken frond**

CLUE C | If the fronds and clusters of spores look like one of these, go to the pages shown.

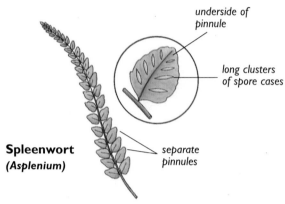

underside of pinnule

long clusters of spore cases

Spleenwort
(Asplenium)

separate pinnules

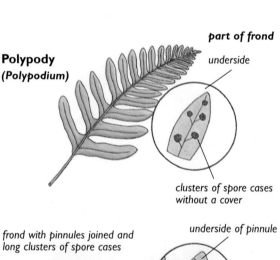

part of frond

Polypody
(Polypodium)

underside

clusters of spore cases without a cover

frond with pinnules joined and long clusters of spore cases

underside of pinnule

Rusty-Back Fern *(Ceterach)*

long clusters of spore cases

UE D If the pinnae of the fronds grow close together on the leaf stalk and the covers of the spore cases are shaped like one of these, go to the page shown.

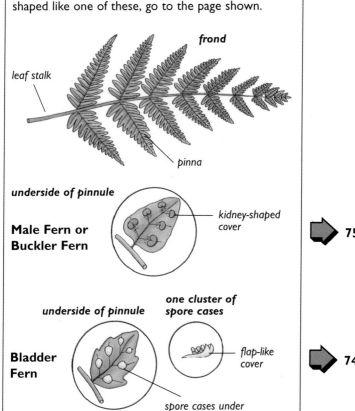

frond

leaf stalk

pinna

underside of pinnule

Male Fern or Buckler Fern

kidney-shaped cover

 75

underside of pinnule

one cluster of spore cases

Bladder Fern

flap-like cover

spore cases under flap-like cover

 74

Shield Fern

round cover

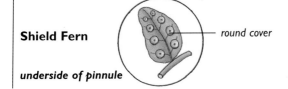 74

underside of pinnule

*frond with
spore cases*

frond with spore cases

leafy frond

Hard Fern
(Blechnum)
(fronds 10–75 cm)
woods, wet heaths
spores June–Aug

*leafy
frond*

Royal Fern
(Osmunda)
(fronds 30–300 cm)
gardens, parks, wet heaths
spores June–Aug

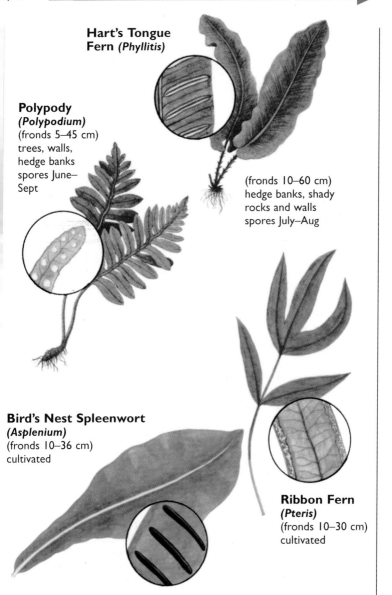

Hart's Tongue Fern *(Phyllitis)*

Polypody
(Polypodium)
(fronds 5–45 cm)
trees, walls,
hedge banks
spores June–
Sept

(fronds 10–60 cm)
hedge banks, shady
rocks and walls
spores July–Aug

Bird's Nest Spleenwort
(Asplenium)
(fronds 10–36 cm)
cultivated

Ribbon Fern
(Pteris)
(fronds 10–30 cm)
cultivated

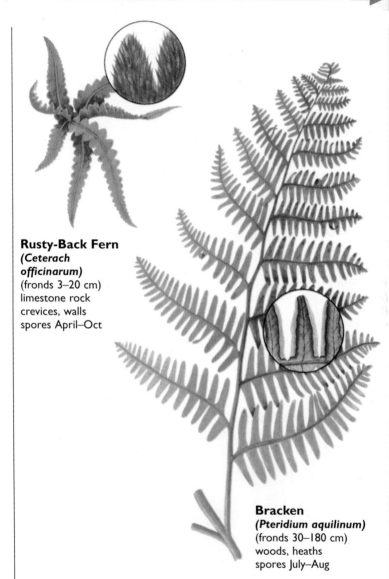

Rusty-Back Fern
(Ceterach officinarum)
(fronds 3–20 cm)
limestone rock
crevices, walls
spores April–Oct

Bracken
(Pteridium aquilinum)
(fronds 30–180 cm)
woods, heaths
spores July–Aug

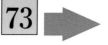

Wall Rue Spleenwort
(Asplenium ruta-muraria)
(fronds 3–12 cm)
walls, rocks
spores June–Oct

Maidenhair Fern
(Adiantum capillus-veneris)
(fronds 10–50 cm)
cultivated

Maidenhair Spleenwort
(Asplenium trichomanes)
(fronds 4–20 cm)
walls, rocks
spores May–Oct

Shield Fern
(Polystichum)
(fronds 30–150 cm)
woods, hedge banks
spores July–Aug

Bladder Fern
(Cystopteris)
(fronds 5–35 cm)
shady rocks, walls
spores July–Aug

Buckler Fern
(Dryopteris) (frond 30–150 cm)
woods, hedge banks, wet heaths
spores July–Sept

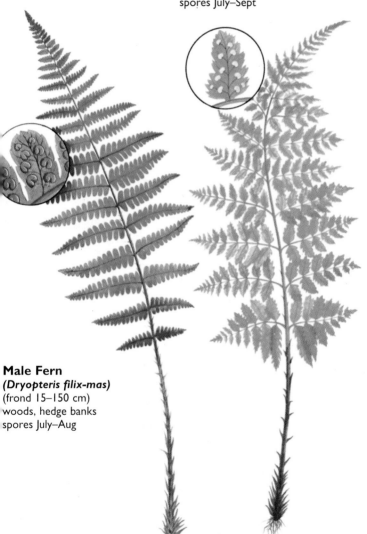

Male Fern
(Dryopteris filix-mas)
(frond 15–150 cm)
woods, hedge banks
spores July–Aug

In early spring the jointed, green stems of Horsetails begin to grow from creeping underground stems. They have whorls of branches.

The leaves form tiny, brown sheaths around the stems at the joints.

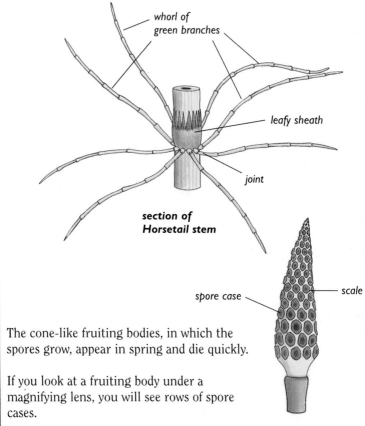

whorl of green branches

leafy sheath

joint

section of Horsetail stem

spore case

scale

The cone-like fruiting bodies, in which the spores grow, appear in spring and die quickly.

If you look at a fruiting body under a magnifying lens, you will see rows of spore cases.

cone-like fruiting body

Horsetails should not be confused with **MARE'S-TAILS**. These unbranched water plants are slightly similar in appearance to Horsetails, but they are flowering plants, with small pink flowers.

If you shake some spores onto a glass slide and look at them under a microscope, you will see the spring-like threads, called **ELATORS**, on them. These help to project the spores into the air. Those that land on suitable ground grow.

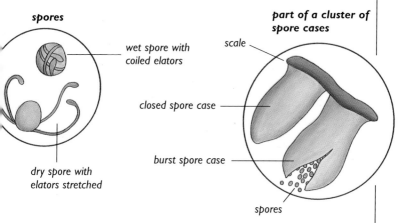

spores

wet spore with coiled elators

dry spore with elators stretched

part of a cluster of spore cases

scale

closed spore case

burst spore case

spores

HOW TO GROW HORSETAILS

If you want to see how Horsetails start to grow, scatter some spores on a piece of sterile clay pot or brick, or damp blotting paper, placed in a container that has a lid.

(To sterilize, boil the piece of clay pot or brick for ten minutes: leave to cool.)

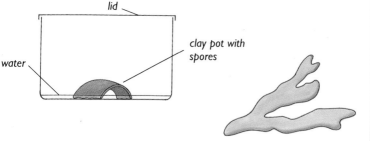

lid

clay pot with spores

water

The Horsetail plant will grow from this.

the first plant (prothallus) 3–4 weeks old

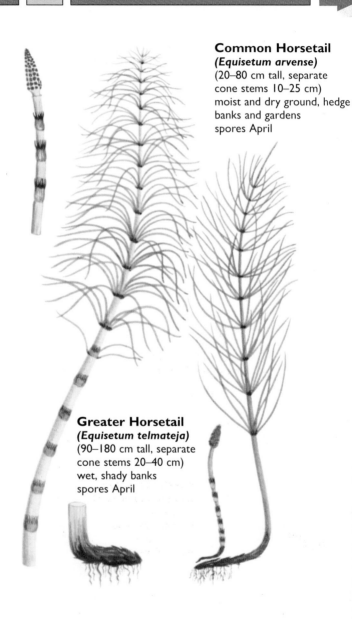

Common Horsetail
(Equisetum arvense)
(20–80 cm tall, separate
cone stems 10–25 cm)
moist and dry ground, hedge
banks and gardens
spores April

Greater Horsetail
(Equisetum telmateja)
(90–180 cm tall, separate
cone stems 20–40 cm)
wet, shady banks
spores April

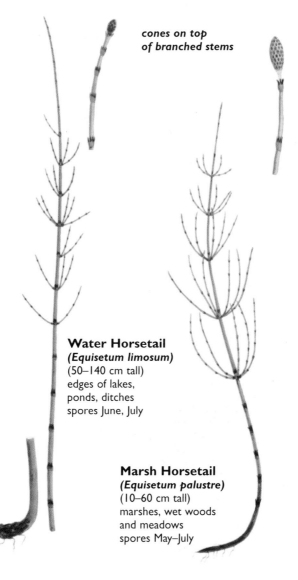

*cones on top
of branched stems*

Water Horsetail
(Equisetum limosum)
(50–140 cm tall)
edges of lakes,
ponds, ditches
spores June, July

Marsh Horsetail
(Equisetum palustre)
(10–60 cm tall)
marshes, wet woods
and meadows
spores May–July

Further Reading

Jordan, Michael, *Encyclopedia of Fungi of Britain and Europe*. David and Charles, 199(
Pentecost, A, *Introduction to Freshwater Algae*. Richmond Publishing Company, 1984
Phillips, Roger, *Mushrooms and Other Fungi of Great Britain and Europe*. Pan Books,
  1981.
Phillips, Roger, *Grasses, Ferns, Mosses and Lichens of Great Britain and Ireland*. Pan
  Books, 1980.

A good way to learn more about the animals and plants in your area is to join
Wildlife Watch, a club for young people interested in wildlife and the environmen
As well as organising activities for its members, Watch produces a national
magazine, local newsletters, and many posters and activity packs. Their address is
Wildlife Watch, The Green, Witham Park, Waterside South, Lincoln LN5 7JR.